TURBULENCE IN GREENBACKS

UNDERSTANDING FINANCIAL SYSTEM FAILINGS

Contents

3

Forward

The monetary framework, a perplexing snare of establishments, markets, and instruments, assumes an essential part in forming the financial scene of countries. It is the lifeblood of commerce, facilitating transactions, allocating capital, and supporting economic expansion. However, beneath the appearance of stability is a history marked by frequent crises, which raises a fundamental question: for what reason does our monetary framework waver?

Characterizing the Monetary Framework

At its center, the monetary framework is an organization of establishments, markets, and mediators that work with the progression of cash and capital. It envelops banks, monetary business sectors, controllers, and different elements that work in show to keep up with liquidity, designate assets proficiently, and alleviate chances. A well-working monetary framework is the key part of a flourishing economy, encouraging venture, business, and development.

The Significance of Soundness

The soundness of the monetary framework is principal for supported financial success. A stable monetary framework gives certainty to financial backers, guarantees the smooth working of installment frameworks, and supports the compelling transmission of money related strategy. Nonetheless, this dependability is definitely not an inborn quality; rather, dependent upon a fragile balance can be disturbed by a horde of variables.

Verifiable Setting: Examples from An earlier time

To understand the reason why our monetary framework frequently flounders, we should look at the illustrations implanted ever. The archives of money are set apart by the scars of past emergencies, from the Economic crisis of the early 20s of the 1930s to the later worldwide monetary emergency of 2008. These episodes act as wake up calls, uncovering weaknesses and disappointments that keep on tormenting the monetary scene.

Underlying Issues: The Mind boggling Web

One conspicuous component adding to the delicacy of the monetary framework is its innate intricacy. Monetary instruments have developed into many-sided substances, frequently unparalleled the understanding of even prepared specialists. This intricacy cultivates obscurity, making it trying to precisely survey gambles. Also, administrative systems battle to stay up with the fast development in monetary business sectors, prompting administrative holes and escape clauses that can be taken advantage of.

Institutional Disappointments: As the primary guardians of financial stability, banks can also act as agents of instability. Additional dangers are posed by the shadow banking industry, which operates outside of traditional banking. Administrative catch, where administrative bodies might be impacted by the elements they should supervise, further subverts the framework's trustworthiness. These institutional disappointments make a shaky place of cards, defenseless to implode under the smallest quake.

Risk The board Disappointments: A Determined Bet

Compelling gamble the board is the bedrock of a versatile monetary framework. Notwithstanding, the quest for benefit in some cases mists judgment, prompting lacking gamble evaluation rehearses. The dangers of a system based on the assumption that markets will always self-correct include asset mispricing and excessive reliance on credit ratings in the lead up to the 2008 crisis.

Social Variables: The Human Element Financial markets are influenced by people. Group attitude, where market members follow the group without autonomous examination, can bring about unreasonable abundance or frenzy selling. Market volatility is amplified and the likelihood of systemic failures is raised by the inherent propensity for excessive risk-taking, which is exacerbated by decision-making that is focused on short-term gain.

Globalization and Interconnectedness: The Cascading type of influence

In a time of globalization, the monetary framework is complicatedly interconnected. Cross-line capital streams can communicate stuns quickly across borders, making a cascading type of influence. Planning global guideline turns into a considerable test, as various purviews wrestle with their remarkable financial real factors and strategy needs.

Government and Strategy Disappointments: Navigating a Precarious situation

The job of legislatures and policymakers in keeping up with monetary security couldn't possibly be more significant. The environment in which the safety nets intended to stabilize the system become strained and porous is created by ineffective monetary policies, fiscal difficulties, and a lack of coordination between the authorities in charge of monetary and fiscal matters.

Mechanical Dangers: The Two sided deal

As innovation progresses, so do the dangers it acquaints with the monetary framework. Online protection dangers pose a potential threat, equipped for upsetting whole monetary organizations. High-recurrence and algorithmic exchanging, while at the same time giving proficiency, likewise present the gamble of fast and unusual market developments.

Social and Monetary Imbalance: A Time Bomb That's Ticking The financial system is tightly woven into the fabric of society. Monetary imbalance, when left neglected, subverts social union as well as enhances monetary dangers. The prohibition of huge portions of the populace from monetary administrations makes a dangerous situation of discontent that can detonate in the midst of emergency.

Changes and Arrangements: Outlining a Course Forward

Despite these difficulties, there is a squeezing need for changes and arrangements. Administrative systems should advance to stay up with monetary development, and hazard the executives practices ought to be supported. Fortifying administration and responsibility, both inside monetary foundations and administrative bodies, is fundamental to remake trust in the framework.

Contextual analyses: Gaining for a fact

Inspecting explicit monetary emergencies, for example, the Reserve funds and Advance emergency of the 1980s or the Asian Monetary Emergency of 1997, gives significant bits of knowledge. Examining the disappointments as well as fruitful recuperation methodologies can offer a guide for exploring future difficulties.

Exploring the Risks

All in all, the delicacy of our monetary framework is an unpredictable embroidery woven from different strings of intricacy, institutional deficiencies, and social elements. Perceiving these weaknesses is the most vital move toward making a stronger monetary design. As we push ahead, the basic lies in gaining from history, embracing changes, and encouraging a monetary framework that fills in as a hearty support point supporting worldwide financial prosperity. The excursion to monetary steadiness is full of difficulties, however the objective is an existence where the monetary framework is an impetus for thriving instead of a wellspring of interminable nervousness.

The historical backdrop of the monetary framework is a narrative set apart by pinnacles of success and valleys of emergency. To comprehend the reasons for the recurrent failures of our financial system, it is essential to examine the historical context. This investigation will dig into key verifiable occasions, each a section in the developing story of monetary business sectors, and concentrate important illustrations that keep on resounding in the present.

The Economic crisis of the early 20s (1929-1939): A Nerve racking Introduction

The Economic crisis of the early 20s, set off by the 1929 securities exchange crash, remains as a fundamental crossroads in monetary history. The breakdown of banks, the dive in modern creation, and taking off joblessness uncovered the weaknesses of an unregulated monetary framework. Illustrations from this time underline the requirement for viable administrative instruments and government mediation to forestall foundational breakdowns.

The Bretton Woods Arrangement (1944): A Post-War Remaking

In the result of The Second Great War, worldwide pioneers gathered at Bretton Woods to plan another global financial request. The subsequent Bretton Woods Understanding laid out a decent conversion standard framework and made the Global Money related Asset (IMF) and the World Bank. While giving solidness, this framework ultimately capitulated to difficulties, highlighting the significance of versatility in monetary designs.

Monetary organizations participated in hazardous loaning works on, prompting the breakdown of various S&L foundations. As a result, regulatory reforms were implemented to emphasize the importance of strict oversight to preserve financial stability.

The Website Air pocket (late 1990s): Unleashed Irrational Exuberance The Dot-Com Bubble of the late 1990s was characterized by an exuberant rise in the valuation of internet-related stocks. The subsequent burst demonstrated the significance of fundamental valuation and the risks associated with speculative zeal. It fills in as a distinct update that market richness, when confined from monetary essentials, can prompt significant market redresses.

The Asian Monetary Emergency (1997): Virus in a Globalized World

The Asian Monetary Emergency showed the hazards of interconnectedness in a globalized economy. Cash downgrades, banking breakdowns, and monetary constrictions in Asian economies resonated all around the world. This emergency highlighted the requirement for composed worldwide reactions and watchful gamble the board in an undeniably interconnected monetary scene.

The Worldwide Monetary Emergency (2008): A Foundational Tidal wave

The latest turning point in monetary history is the Worldwide Monetary Emergency (GFC) of 2008. Filled by subprime contract loaning, complex monetary instruments, and deficient gamble evaluations, the emergency prompted the breakdown of major monetary foundations and a serious financial slump. Illustrations from the GFC stress the basic job of straightforwardness, risk alleviation, and the interconnectedness of worldwide monetary business sectors.

Illustrations Learned

On the whole, these verifiable occasions uncover an intermittent example of monetary overabundances, administrative slips, and fundamental weaknesses. The significance of proactive guideline, risk the executives, and flexibility to changing financial scenes arises as a consistent idea. Moreover, the worldwide idea of current money requires global collaboration and coordination in creating viable arrangements.

Suggestions for the Present and Future

The illustrations gathered from verifiable monetary emergencies act as guideposts for exploring the difficulties of the present and future. Regulators, policymakers, and market participants must remain vigilant as financial systems continue to change. The financial landscape of today is interconnected, necessitating a global perspective that emphasizes the necessity of collaborative efforts to address emerging risks.

In disentangling the embroidery of monetary history, we track down a story rich with wins and hardships. The examples from the Economic crisis of the early 20s, Bretton Woods, Reserve funds and Credit Emergency, Website Air pocket, Asian Monetary Emergency, and the Worldwide Monetary Emergency aggregately shape how we might interpret the delicacy inborn in monetary frameworks. As we explore the intricacies of the present and graph a course for the future, a careful thought of these verifiable sections is fundamental for strengthen the monetary framework against the vulnerabilities that lie ahead. The reverberations of the past coax us to be cautious overseers of monetary strength, guaranteeing that the mix-ups of history act as reference points, directing us from the cliff of foundational disappointment.

Intricacy and Haziness: The Tangled Web

The monetary framework's development has been set apart by a rising intricacy of monetary instruments and exchanges. Subordinates, securitization, and algorithmic exchanging, while expected to improve productivity, have made a snare of intricacy that difficulties market members' comprehension. These intricate financial instruments can create an atmosphere that is ripe for erroneous predictions and judgments because of their opaque nature, which can make it difficult to see the true risks involved.

Absence of Straightforwardness in Monetary Business sectors: The Cloak of Vulnerability

Straightforwardness is the bedrock of confidence in monetary business sectors. However, a significant risk is posed by the absence of transparency, particularly in complex derivatives markets and over-the-counter (OTC) markets. Financial backers might know nothing about the genuine dangers they are presented to, and market members might battle to measure the monetary soundness of counterparties. Because uncertainty breeds fear, this opacity can amplify market panic during times of crisis.

Administrative Holes and Escape clauses: A Place of Cards Holding on to Fall

The administrative structure is planned to be the wellbeing net that forestalls fundamental disappointments. In any case, the fast development of monetary business sectors frequently outperforms administrative transformation. Administrative holes and provisos permit elements to participate in exercises that fall outside the domain of oversight.

The notorious "shadow banking" area, working on the edges of customary guideline, embodies how these holes can make a place of cards, where dangers gather inconspicuous until an emergency uncovered the delicacy.

Interconnectedness of Monetary Organizations: The Cascading type of influence

Monetary organizations are the mainstays of the monetary framework, yet their interconnectedness can be a blade that cuts both ways. Enormous organizations frequently take part in complex organizations of exchanges and conditions. At the point when one establishment flounders, it can set off a cascading type of influence, spreading trouble all through the framework. Individual failures become systemic risks as a result of the interconnectedness, which amplifies their impact.

Primary Issues and the 2008 Worldwide Monetary Emergency

The Worldwide Monetary Emergency of 2008 fills in as a distinct delineation of how primary issues can prompt a fundamental breakdown. Complex home loan supported protections, entwined worldwide monetary foundations, and deficient gamble evaluations finished in a staggering monetary implosion. The result provoked a reexamination of the monetary framework's construction, featuring the dire requirement for changes to address these primary weaknesses.

Returning to Administrative Systems: Towards a Tough Construction

Resolving primary issues requires a diverse methodology. Administrative structures should develop to stay up with monetary advancement, shutting existing holes and expecting new dangers. Expanded straightforwardness, particularly in complex monetary instruments, can enable market members to pursue informed choices. Moreover, endeavors to lessen the interconnectedness of monetary organizations through judicious gamble the board practices can moderate the foundational chances related with huge scope disappointments.

Worldwide Coordination in Guideline: Separating Storehouses

The worldwide idea of monetary business sectors requires global participation in administrative endeavors. Standards can be harmonised, regulatory arbitrage can be prevented, and the global financial system can become more cohesive through coordination between regulatory bodies in different jurisdictions. Drives, for example, the Monetary Steadiness Board (FSB) assume a significant part in encouraging this coordination, guaranteeing that primary issues are tended to on a worldwide scale.

Innovation and Underlying Development: Opportunities and

dangers Despite the fact that technology has made the financial system more complicated, it also holds the key to fixing some structural problems. Headways in fintech, administrative innovation (RegTech), and dispersed record innovation (DLT) offer chances to improve straightforwardness, smooth out administrative consistence, and make stronger monetary frameworks. In any case, the reception of these advances should be joined by hearty gamble the executives to forestall potentially negative side-effects.

: Building an Establishment for Security

In unwinding the primary issues inside the monetary framework, it becomes clear that the mission for solidness is a continuous excursion. Intricacy, obscurity, and administrative weaknesses are difficulties that request persistent consideration and variation. By resolving these underlying issues head-on, through administrative changes, upgraded straightforwardness, and worldwide coordination, we can establish the groundwork for a monetary framework that isn't just versatile in that frame of mind of shocks yet additionally equipped for cultivating maintainable financial development. Modern finance's inherent complexity need not make people vulnerable; rather, they can be changed into qualities through smart and proactive measures.

What Banks Do: Gatekeepers or Modelers of Emergency?

Banks, as the foundation of the monetary framework, are depended with the obligation of defending stores, working with exchanges, and judiciously overseeing gambles. Notwithstanding, history uncovers cases where banks have wandered from this command, participating in dangerous loaning rehearses and theoretical endeavors. The Reserve funds and Credit Emergency of the 1980s in the US fills in as a strong model, where remiss guideline and unwise loaning prompted the breakdown of various reserve funds and credit establishments, leaving citizens with a heavy bailout bill.

Private Banking: Exploring the Outskirts

The rise of the shadow banking area, working past the conventional administrative structure, represents a special arrangement of difficulties. Organizations inside this shadow domain, including mutual funds and non-bank monetary elements, frequently participate in exercises like conventional banks yet with less administrative imperatives. The 2008 Worldwide Monetary Emergency uncovered the weakness of this area, with the breakdown of Lehman Siblings highlighting the dangers related with elements working in the shadows.

Administrative Catch: At the point when Watchmen Become Partners

Administrative bodies are intended to go about as gatekeepers, guaranteeing that monetary foundations comply with reasonable practices and comply to guidelines. Notwithstanding, the idea of administrative catch uncovers a disturbing dynamic where administrative bodies might turn out to be excessively firmly lined up with the elements they should regulate. This comfortable relationship can prompt a debilitating of administrative oversight, as controllers might be impacted by the very organizations they are intended to police. Lax regulatory oversight allowed risky practices to flourish unchecked in the lead-up to the 2008 financial crisis, demonstrating the effects of regulatory capture.

Motivational Systems and Moral Danger: The Causes of Failure Incorrect incentive structures that encourage excessive risk-taking are frequently the root causes of institutional failure. These problems are made worse by the idea of moral hazard, in which institutions take risks knowing that they will be saved in the event of failure. The Too Huge to Even consider fizzling (TBTF) issue, featured during the 2008 emergency, embodies how establishments considered crucial for the monetary framework might participate in more hazardous way of behaving, certain that they will be safeguarded from the outcomes.

Taking Care of Institutional Weaknesses: Reforms to the law To prevent institutional failures, a two-pronged strategy is required: supporting administrative oversight and rebuilding motivator frameworks. Comprehensive regulatory reforms must address gaps that permit excessive risk-taking, increase transparency, and cultivate a culture of accountability within financial institutions.

Improving Gamble The board Practices: Exploring the Unexplored world

Powerful gamble the board is a foundation of institutional strength. Establishments should embrace strong gamble appraisal rehearses, stress testing, and situation examination to expect and explore likely difficulties. Gaining from past disappointments, monetary organizations ought to focus on a forward-looking way to deal with risk the board that goes past consistence to cultivate a certified obligation to solidness.

Reinforcing Administration and Responsibility: A Cultural Shift Institutional flaws are more than just technical errors; They frequently result from organizational cultural flaws. Fortifying administration structures, guaranteeing board freedom, and advancing a culture of responsibility are fundamental parts of building versatile foundations. Sheets and leaders should be considered responsible for their choices, and a solid moral establishment ought to be imbued in the hierarchical culture.

Contextual investigations: Lessons from the Field Investigating specific case studies, such as the demise of Long-Term Capital Management (LTCM) and Enron, provides useful insights into the underlying dynamics of institutional failure. Examining these cases recognizes designs, main drivers, and compelling systems for recuperation and change.

Conclusion: A Call for Watchfulness and Change

Organizations are the mainstays of the monetary framework, and their disappointments can send shockwaves through economies. Perceiving the weaknesses innate in institutional designs is the most vital move toward building a stronger monetary scene. We can work toward ensuring that institutions perform their intended function as custodians of financial stability rather than architects of crisis by implementing regulatory reforms, improving risk management practices, and instituting a culture shift toward accountability. The excursion toward a powerful monetary framework requires an aggregate obligation to gaining from previous oversights and cultivating a culture that focuses on reasonability, straightforwardness, and moral direct.

Risk The board Disappointments Presentation

Risk the board is the foundation of a stable monetary framework, giving the compass that guides establishments through the erratic waters of financial unpredictability. Nonetheless, the archives of monetary history uncover cases where this compass neglected to work sufficiently, prompting devastating results. This investigation digs into the intricacies of hazard the executives disappointments, inspecting the entanglements of deficient gamble appraisal, the mispricing of resources, and the overreliance using a credit card evaluations.

Deficient Gamble Appraisal Practices: An Imperfect Compass

At the core of hazard the executives disappointments lies the test of precisely surveying and evaluating gambles. Monetary foundations, driven by the quest for benefit, may surrender to the allurement of making light of dangers or underrating the possible effect of unfriendly occasions. The 2008 Worldwide Monetary Emergency fills in as an unmistakable representation, with monetary organizations underrating the dangers related with subprime contract loaning, prompting a flowing impact that resounded all through the worldwide monetary framework.

Mispricing of Resources: The Delusion of Significant worth

The mispricing of resources, a result of imperfect gamble evaluation and market richness, can make a hallucination of significant worth that at last vanishes when financial real factors set in. The Website Air pocket of the last part of the 1990s and the ensuing burst uncovered how market extravagance can prompt expanded resource costs, just to be trailed by a sharp revision. The misalignment among saw and inborn worth features the risks of depending on market opinion without a strong groundwork of chance administration standards.

Overreliance On layaway Evaluations: A House Built on Sand
In the 2008 financial crisis, credit rating agencies were tasked with assessing the creditworthiness of financial institutions and instruments. Overreliance using a credit card evaluations, without free examination, drove financial backers to put unjustifiable

confidence in complex monetary items, for example, contract upheld protections, which were eventually uncovered to be far more hazardous than their credit scores proposed. The aftermath uncovered a foundational disappointment in risk the board, where the elastic stepping of reliability added to a misguided sensation that all is well and good.

Conduct Predispositions in Hazard The executives: The Human Component

Risk the board isn't just a specialized discipline yet additionally a mental one. Overconfidence, herd mentality, and anchoring are examples of behavioral biases that can impair judgment and result in poor decisions regarding risk management. The Drawn out Capital Administration (LTCM) emergency in the last part of the 1990s represents how the splendor of Nobel laureates in financial matters was eclipsed by pomposity, eventually bringing about a tremendous disappointment that required an organized bailout to deflect a fundamental implosion.

Risk of Market Liquidity: Concealed Propensities

Market liquidity risk, frequently underrated in times of monetary solidness, can surface suddenly during seasons of pressure. The 2020 Corona virus pandemic displayed how an apparently hearty monetary framework can confront liquidity challenges when defied with unanticipated shocks. Establishments, caught off guard for the unexpected dissipation of market liquidity, wrestled with the outcomes, featuring the requirement for a more nuanced comprehension of liquidity risk in risk the board systems.

Problems with Risk Management: A Comprehensive Methodology

Tending to take a chance with the executives disappointments requires an exhaustive and comprehensive methodology that includes both specialized and conduct perspectives.

Enhanced Stress Testing and Risk Modeling: Building Strength

Risk displaying should develop to integrate a more extensive scope of situations, including tail dangers and dark swan occasions. Stress testing, a basic part of chance administration, ought to go past administrative necessities to recreate outrageous situations and evaluate an organization's flexibility under unfavorable circumstances. These actions guarantee that risk the executives structures are adequately strong to endure unexpected difficulties.

Advancing Gamble Culture: From Consistence to Responsibility

Risk the executives isn't simply a bunch of systems; It is an organizational mindset that is ingrained at every level. Organizations should develop a gamble mindful culture that focuses on judiciousness, straightforwardness, and a pledge to the drawn out wellbeing of the establishment. Employees will be given the freedom to express their concerns without fear of retaliation as part of this cultural shift by aligning incentives with risk management objectives, encouraging open communication about risks, and so forth.

Expansion and Portfolio Supporting: Guardrails against Fundamental Disappointment

Expansion stays a crucial gamble the board system. Diversifying their portfolios across different asset classes, regions, and investment strategies is a good way for institutions to avoid concentration risks. Furthermore, portfolio supporting procedures, like utilizing subsidiaries to moderate explicit dangers, can go about as guardrails against the foundational disappointment that can result from a concentrated gamble openness.

The Job of Administrative Oversight: A Difficult exercise

Administrative bodies assume a vital part in laying out the system for risk the executives rehearses. However, the regulatory environment ought to strike a delicate balance between ensuring that institutions adhere to prudent risk management principles and avoiding excessive constraints that stifle innovation. Administrative oversight ought to advance close by the monetary scene, adjusting to new difficulties and arising gambles.

Conclusion: Exploring What's to come

As we explore the future, the examples from risk the board disappointments highlight the requirement for ceaseless watchfulness and transformation. The monetary framework is innately unique, formed by a many-sided interaction of financial powers, innovative headways, and human way of behaving. By gaining from verifiable disappointments, upgrading risk the board systems, and cultivating a culture of versatility, the monetary business can construct an establishment that endures the vulnerabilities of tomorrow. The excursion towards viable gamble the board is a never-ending one, requiring a promise to learning, development, and an unfaltering devotion to the rules that support monetary steadiness.

Introduction to Behavioral Factors

Although the financial system is frequently portrayed as a realm of numbers, algorithms, and economic theories, the intricacies of human behavior have a significant impact. Conduct factors assume a crucial part in molding market elements, financial backer choices, and, eventually, the solidness of the monetary framework. This investigation digs into the social subtleties, looking at the effect of crowd mindset, unreasonable gamble taking, and the commonness of short-termism in navigation.

Group Mindset: The Protected, closed off environment of Business sectors

Crowd mindset, a peculiarity where people follow the activities of the greater part, can make a self-supporting criticism circle in monetary business sectors. During times of extravagance, this aggregate conduct fills resource bubbles, driving costs to impractical levels. On the other hand, during seasons of frenzy, group conduct can prompt mass selling, worsening business sector slumps. Contextual investigations, like the Website Air pocket and ensuing burst, represent how crowd attitude can intensify market instability and add to foundational chances.

Excessive Behavior of Taking Risks: Moving on the Verge

The quest for benefit frequently allures market members to participate in exorbitant gamble taking way of behaving. Monetary organizations, driven by the commitment of exceptional yields, may embrace dangerous endeavors without completely grasping the expected disadvantages. The 2008 Worldwide Monetary Emergency exposed the outcomes of this way of behaving, as the confusion of dangers related with subprime contracts prompted an outpouring of disappointments and a serious financial slump. Understanding the mental underpinnings of hazard taking way of behaving is urgent for alleviating foundational weaknesses.

Short-Termism in Direction: Chasing Immediate Gains Market participants prioritize immediate gains over long-term stability, posing a systemic risk due to the prevalence of short-termism in financial decision-making. Quarterly income pressures, extra designs attached to momentary execution, and the steady investigation of stock costs add to a nearsighted spotlight on transient outcomes.

Pomposity and Mental Predispositions: The Vulnerable sides

Pomposity and mental predispositions, inborn in human navigation, present vulnerable sides that can prompt imperfect decisions. The Long-Term Capital Management (LTCM) crisis at the end of the 1990s exemplifies how even highly educated people can become overconfident. Perceiving the effect of mental predispositions, for example, tendency to look for predictable answers and mooring, is fundamental for planning risk the executives methodologies that record for the innate limits of human discernment.

Conduct Variables in Market Frenzies: Dread and Disease

Market panics, described by silly selling and a fast decrease in resource costs, are much of the time energized by conduct factors like trepidation and virus. The 2008 Worldwide Monetary Emergency saw dread spreading through monetary business sectors, prompting a breakdown in trust and liquidity. Conduct virus, where alarm in one market spreads to other people, features the interconnectedness of worldwide monetary frameworks and the requirement for components to treat unreasonable way of behaving during emergencies.

Tending to Conduct Variables: A Conduct Financial matters Focal point

Understanding and tending to conduct factors in the monetary framework requires a multidisciplinary approach, drawing bits of knowledge from social financial matters.

Conduct Financial aspects in Guideline: Poking Toward Reasonability

Administrative bodies can use bits of knowledge from conduct financial matters to plan mediations that prod market members toward more reasonable way of behaving. For instance, revelation prerequisites, cautioning marks, and default choices that line up with long haul monetary wellbeing can assist with checking the effect of mental predispositions and short-termism.

Awareness and instruction: Enlightening the Conduct Scene

Upgrading monetary education and advancing consciousness of social inclinations are urgent parts of alleviating fundamental dangers. A more informed and resilient financial ecosystem can be created by educating investors, financial professionals, and policymakers about the psychological factors that influence decision-making.

Motivation Designs and Corporate Administration: Adjusting Interests to Solidness

Realigning motivation designs to remunerate long haul execution and reasonable gamble the board is fundamental. Corporate administration rehearses that focus on straightforwardness, responsibility, and an emphasis on maintainable worth creation can assist with moderating the effect of conduct factors on dynamic inside monetary organizations.

Innovative Arrangements: Increasing Human Direction

Progressions in innovation, especially man-made reasoning (simulated intelligence) and AI, offer chances to expand human navigation by distinguishing and alleviating social predispositions. Algorithmic devices can examine immense datasets and give leaders bits of knowledge that go past human mental capacities.

Conclusion: Navigating the Behavioral Seas The financial system is shaped by a variety of complex behavioral factors. Exploring these oceans requires a nuanced comprehension of human way of behaving, a pledge to continuous schooling, and a proactive way to deal with planning frameworks that moderate the effect of conduct inclinations. As we steer through the eccentric waters of monetary business sectors, perceiving the job of brain research in navigation is definitely not an indication of shortcoming yet a commonsense affirmation that human way of behaving is a necessary and persuasive power in the mind boggling embroidery of the monetary framework. By tending to social variables, we can endeavor to construct a monetary biological system that isn't just proficient yet in addition strong notwithstanding the mind boggling exchange among judiciousness and human brain research.

Globalization and Interconnectedness Presentation

The advanced monetary scene is portrayed by an exceptional degree of interconnectivity and globalization. While these highlights have introduced a period of expanded effectiveness and admittance to capital, they have likewise presented new components of intricacy and chance. This investigation digs into the complicated trap of globalization and interconnectedness in the monetary framework, investigating the elements of cross-line capital streams, the disease impacts in worldwide business sectors, and the difficulties in organizing worldwide guideline.

Cross-Boundary Capital Streams: The Liquid Cash of Worldwide Money

Globalization has worked with the smooth motion of capital across borders, empowering ventures to rise above geological limits. While this interconnectedness upgrades capital effectiveness and supports monetary development, it additionally opens countries to the dangers related with unexpected changes in financial backer feeling. The Asian Monetary Emergency of 1997 fills in as an unmistakable sign of how cross-line capital streams can change limited financial issues into worldwide difficulties, enhancing the speed and force of monetary virus.

Virus Impacts in Worldwide Business sectors: The Cascading type of influence

The interconnected idea of worldwide monetary business sectors implies that aggravations in a single district can have flowing impacts around the world. Monetary disease, where shocks spread quickly across borders, epitomizes the inborn dangers of interconnectivity. The 2008 Worldwide Monetary Emergency showed how the breakdown of major monetary foundations in the US resounded universally, causing a synchronized financial slump. Understanding the systems of virus is critical for making successful gamble the board procedures in a universally associated monetary environment.

Challenges in Organizing Global Guideline: The Administrative Mosaic

As monetary exercises length different wards, the requirement for global collaboration in guideline becomes principal. In any case, accomplishing orchestrated administrative norms across assorted economies presents critical difficulties. Administrative dissimilarity and holes in oversight can set out open doors for administrative exchange, where monetary foundations exploit contrasts in administrative systems for their potential benefit. The mission for compelling worldwide guideline includes exploring these difficulties to construct an administrative system that is both vigorous and versatile.

The Job of Worldwide Establishments: Exploring Intricacy

Worldwide foundations, like the Worldwide Money related Asset (IMF) and the Monetary Steadiness Board (FSB), assume a crucial part in cultivating worldwide joint effort and tending to difficulties emerging from globalization. These foundations give gatherings to discourse, work with the trading of data, and add to the improvement of all around the world composed approaches. Nonetheless, the viability of these establishments relies on the eagerness of part countries to team up and carry out settled upon measures.

Money Dangers and Conversion scale Unpredictability: A Situation with two sides

The commonness of various monetary forms in worldwide exchange presents money dangers and swapping scale unpredictability. While a different arrangement of monetary forms gives adaptability, it likewise opens market members to vacillations that can influence the worth of speculations. The Asian Monetary Emergency featured how weak economies with critical outer obligation in unfamiliar monetary forms can confront extreme difficulties during times of cash deterioration. Overseeing money gambles becomes critical for the two financial backers and policymakers in a universally interconnected monetary framework.

Mechanical Headways and Worldwide Money: Speeding up Interconnectedness

Mechanical progressions, especially in fintech and advanced finance, further speed up the interconnectedness of the worldwide monetary framework. Advanced stages empower prompt cross-line exchanges, lessening contact in worldwide monetary streams. Be that as it may, the fast reception of innovation likewise presents new difficulties, including network safety dangers and the potential for market interruptions through algorithmic exchanging. Adjusting the advantages of mechanical advancement with the dangers it presents requires careful oversight and versatile administrative structures.

Sovereign Obligation Emergencies: A Worldwide Test

Sovereign obligation emergencies, for example, those saw in Europe during the Eurozone emergency, highlight how interconnectedness enhances the effect of monetary difficulties. The infection impacts of a sovereign default can spread quickly across borders, influencing adjoining economies as well as worldwide monetary business sectors. Cooperative endeavors in overseeing sovereign obligation challenges require coordination between countries, global foundations, and confidential leasers.

End: Cruising the Worldwide Monetary Oceans

As we explore the worldwide monetary oceans, the transaction of globalization and interconnectedness presents the two amazing open doors and difficulties. Perceiving the dangers related with cross-line capital streams, disease impacts, and administrative intricacies is fundamental for creating strong monetary frameworks. Worldwide joint effort, worked with by worldwide organizations, mechanical developments, and versatile administrative structures, turns into the compass directing countries through the intricacies of an internationally interconnected monetary biological system. The excursion includes tracking down a sensitive equilibrium that tackles the advantages of globalization while moderating the dangers, guaranteeing that the interconnected monetary framework adds to worldwide flourishing as opposed to being a wellspring of foundational weakness.

Government and Strategy Disappointments

Presentation

States and their strategies assume a significant part in forming the administrative scene and guaranteeing the solidness of the monetary framework. Nonetheless, history is packed with cases where government activities, or inactions, have added to monetary emergencies and foundational disappointments. Regulatory lapses, moral hazard, and the difficulties of achieving the right balance between intervention and market forces are all examined in this investigation into the complexities of financial policy and government failures.

Regulative Delays: The tragic flaw of Oversight

Viable guideline is the foundation of a stable monetary framework, yet administrative failures have been repetitive wellsprings of weakness. The Reserve funds and Credit Emergency during the 1980s and the 2008 Worldwide Monetary Emergency both spotlight occasions where administrative oversight missed the mark, permitting dangerous practices to thrive. For strengthening the regulatory framework, it is essential to comprehend the underlying causes of regulatory lapses, such as inadequate resources, regulatory capture, or the difficulties of overseeing rapidly evolving financial instruments.

Moral Danger: The Inconspicuous Hand of Government Certifications

Government mediations, especially as bailouts, can unintentionally make moral peril — a circumstance where foundations face over the top challenges with the conviction that they will be saved from the results of disappointment.

Procyclical Approaches: Powering the Fire of Wins and Fails

Government approaches, when ineffectively aligned, can fuel the repetitive idea of monetary business sectors. Procyclical strategies, which enhance monetary patterns, can add to the development of resource rises during times of financial extension and extend slumps during constrictions. The Website Air pocket and the ensuing burst give experiences into how strategies that coincidentally fuel market extravagance can plant the seeds of a resulting emergency, requiring a reassessment of the job of countercyclical measures.

Financial Approach and Gravity: The Tightrope of Public Money

Monetary strategy choices, particularly during times of monetary slumps, can shape the direction of monetary security. The discussion among boost and gravity estimates in the fallout of the 2008 emergency outlines the difficulties of tracking down the right equilibrium. While boost estimates expect to restore monetary action, unreasonable starkness can smother development, prompting a delayed time of financial difficulty. Making compelling monetary strategies requires a far reaching comprehension of the financial setting and an acknowledgment of the interconnectedness between open money and monetary security.

Global Coordination Difficulties: The Worldwide Riddle

In an interconnected world, planning strategies across countries is an imposing test. Different public interests, administrative systems, and monetary circumstances can obstruct cooperative endeavors to resolve worldwide monetary issues. The coordination challenges were clear during the Eurozone emergency, where dissimilar monetary strategies and the shortfall of a bound together methodology confounded endeavors to by and large purpose the emergency. Exploring the worldwide monetary scene requires encouraging global collaboration and creating instruments for composed reactions to fundamental difficulties.

The Job of Government in Encouraging Advancement: A Situation with two sides

Government strategies likewise impact monetary advancement, which can either upgrade effectiveness or present new dangers. The ascent of perplexing monetary instruments and the appearance of fintech epitomize the double idea of monetary development. While encouraging advancement is critical for the development of the monetary framework, policymakers should simultaneously survey and deal with the potential dangers that creative practices might present.

Conclusion: Outlining a Course for Versatility

Government and strategy disappointments in the monetary framework are wake up calls that highlight the requirement for smart, versatile, and facilitated policymaking. Gaining from verifiable slips up, policymakers should persistently reconsider administrative systems, figure out some kind of harmony in money related and monetary approach choices, and cultivate worldwide coordinated effort to explore the intricacies of the worldwide monetary environment. The excursion toward monetary flexibility requests a promise to rules that focus on security, responsibility, and a profound comprehension of the multifaceted exchange between government activities and the wellbeing of the monetary framework.

Innovative Dangers

Presentation

The fast development of innovation has changed the monetary scene, presenting extraordinary productivity, advancement, and interconnectedness. However, financial institutions, regulators, and policymakers must navigate a new frontier of risks brought about by technological advancements. This investigation digs into the mechanical dangers intrinsic in the monetary framework, going from network protection dangers and algorithmic weaknesses to the difficulties presented by arising advancements like blockchain and man-made consciousness.

Network protection Dangers: Cybersecurity threats loom large as a pervasive risk in an age when digital data storage and transactions are the norm. Defending the Digital Fortress Monetary organizations are ideal objectives for cyberattacks, going from information breaks and ransomware to complex hacking endeavors.

Algorithmic Weaknesses: Unwinding the Code

The rising dependence on calculations for exchanging, risk the executives, and navigation presents the gamble of algorithmic weaknesses. Errors, bugs, or potentially negative side-effects in algorithmic codes can prompt unexpected and extreme market disturbances, as seen in streak crashes. The perplexing and frequently murky nature of calculations enhances the test of distinguishing and alleviating expected chances. Thorough testing, constant observing, and straightforward divulgence are basic to alleviate the dangers related with algorithmic weaknesses.

Arising Advancements: The Blade that cuts both ways

While arising advances, for example, blockchain, man-made consciousness (simulated intelligence), and appropriated record innovation hold huge commitment for reforming the monetary business, they additionally present novel dangers.

Blockchain's decentralized nature can challenge conventional administrative structures, expecting transformations to guarantee consistence. Man-made intelligence, while upgrading dynamic cycles, achieves forward worries inclination, responsibility, and the moral utilization of information. Exploring the double idea of these innovations requires a reasonable methodology that saddles their true capacity while relieving related chances.

Functional Dangers: Beyond the Digital Facade The digitalization of financial services entails operational risks, such as system outages, disruptions in technology infrastructure, and platform failures. The reliance on interconnected systems raises the risk of a chain of operational failures that can have an effect on multiple institutions at once. Building versatile mechanical foundation, consolidating overt repetitiveness measures, and creating hearty emergency courses of action are pivotal to tending to functional dangers in the advanced time.

Administrative Difficulties: Adjusting to the Speed of Advancement

Controllers face the overwhelming errand of staying up with the quick development of innovation. The test lies in making guidelines that cultivate advancement without compromising customer security, market trustworthiness, and monetary dependability. Finding some kind of harmony requires a proactive methodology, joint effort between industry partners and controllers, and an administrative system that can adjust to the powerful scene of innovative headways.

Information Security Concerns: Adjusting Advancement and Assurance

As monetary establishments influence tremendous measures of information for examination, personalization, and chance administration, worries about information protection strengthen. Finding some kind of harmony between outfitting the advantages of information driven development and shielding individual protection is a basic test. Administrative systems like GDPR (General Information Insurance Guideline) highlight the developing significance of guaranteeing straightforward and moral information rehearses inside the monetary area.

Interconnectedness and Foundational Dangers: The Organization Impact

The interconnected idea of the monetary environment, worked with by innovation, presents foundational gambles. A disturbance in one piece of the organization might possibly flow through interconnected frameworks, enhancing the effect. The interconnectedness of monetary establishments, fintech firms, and market members requires an all encompassing comprehension of the organization impact and the improvement of components to moderate fundamental dangers emerging from innovative disturbances.

Conclusion: Protecting the Computerized Outskirts

Mechanical dangers in the monetary framework are natural for the computerized period, requiring an exhaustive and versatile way to deal with risk the board. Monetary organizations, controllers, and policymakers should team up to sustain network protection guards, address algorithmic weaknesses, and explore the intricacies presented by arising innovations. By embracing development while focusing on risk relief, the monetary business can explore the computerized boondocks with flexibility and certainty, guaranteeing that innovation stays an empowering influence instead of a wellspring of fundamental weakness.

Social and Monetary Imbalance Presentation

The monetary scene isn't just formed by financial powers yet in addition profoundly affected by friendly elements. The steady issues of social and monetary disparity present huge difficulties for the monetary framework, affecting admittance to assets, open doors, and the general dependability of economies. This investigation digs into the multi-layered parts of social and monetary imbalance, analyzing variations in abundance, monetary consideration, and the job of monetary foundations in alleviating or worsening these partitions.

Abundance Incongruities: The Gap Enlarges

The collection of abundance is a critical driver of social and monetary imbalance. Variations in pay and abundance dissemination, frequently powered by foundational factors, add to the developing hole between the princely and the underestimated. The grouping of abundance among a chosen handful cutoff points monetary versatility as well as postures dangers to monetary soundness, as an unbalanced effect on monetary business sectors can prompt speculative air pockets and market bends.

Monetary Incorporation: Opening Financial Potential

Admittance to monetary administrations is a basic consider tending to social and financial imbalance. The unbanked and underbanked populaces, frequently barred from standard monetary frameworks, face difficulties in building resources, getting to credit, and getting their monetary prospects. Overcoming any barrier in monetary consideration requires creative methodologies, for example, fintech arrangements and comprehensive financial practices, to guarantee that everybody has the amazing chance to take part in and benefit from the monetary framework.

Fundamental Segregation: Breaking Obstructions

Fundamental segregation, whether in light of race, orientation, or other financial elements, sustains imbalance inside the monetary framework. Predispositions in loaning rehearses, wage holes, and restricted portrayal in positions of authority prevent the monetary advancement of minimized networks. Monetary foundations assume a critical part in destroying these boundaries by embracing comprehensive strategies, advancing variety, and effectively tending to biased rehearses.

Schooling Gap: Enabling Through Information

Schooling partition fuels social and monetary imbalance, as variations in admittance to quality training influence future procuring potential and monetary proficiency. Overcoming this issue requires designated endeavors to upgrade monetary schooling, guaranteeing that people from all foundations have the information and abilities to settle on informed monetary choices. Monetary organizations can contribute by supporting instructive drives that engage people to explore the intricacies of the monetary scene.

Lodging Inconsistencies: The Groundwork of Imbalance

Admittance to reasonable lodging is a foundation of monetary security, yet lodging variations persevere, especially in metropolitan regions. Biased loaning practices, improvement, and deficient lodging arrangements add to inconsistent admittance to lodging open doors. Tending to lodging inconsistencies includes exhaustive strategy measures, including reasonable lodging drives, hostile to separation guidelines, and local area improvement endeavors to establish comprehensive and manageable living conditions.

Corporate Social Obligation: Past Benefit Expansion

Monetary establishments bear an obligation to add to social and financial value through corporate social obligation (CSR) drives. By adjusting strategic approaches to moral guidelines, advancing local area venture, and cultivating reasonable turn of events, monetary establishments can effectively take part in restricting social and financial partitions. CSR endeavors ought to go past benefit amplification, perceiving the more extensive effect that monetary foundations have on the prosperity of society.

Government Strategies: Making a Comprehensive System

Government strategies assume a crucial part in forming the financial scene. Moderate expense strategies, social security nets, and designated intercessions can relieve imbalance and make a more level battleground. Policymakers ought to endeavor to institute estimates that advance comprehensive monetary development, address fundamental separation, and guarantee that monetary frameworks work to help all residents.

Worldwide Viewpoints: Connecting Global Imbalance

Social and monetary imbalance are not bound to public lines; they manifest all around the world. Resolving these issues requires worldwide participation, as worldwide monetary frameworks, exchange strategies, and improvement drives fundamentally impact the dissemination of abundance on a worldwide scale. Cooperative endeavors to diminish worldwide monetary incongruities can add to an additional fair and impartial world.

Decision: Fashioning a Way to Correspondence

Spanning social and monetary disparity in the monetary scene requests an aggregate responsibility from monetary foundations, policymakers, and society at large. By tending to abundance incongruities, upgrading monetary consideration, destroying foundational separation, and taking on mindful strategic policies, the monetary framework can turn into an impetus for positive social change. As we explore these difficulties, the quest for balance ought to be at the front of monetary systems, approaches, and drives, guaranteeing that the advantages of financial development are shared fairly across different networks and socioeconomics.

Changes and Arrangements Presentation

Tending to the diverse difficulties of the monetary framework requires striking changes and creative arrangements. This investigation delves into important areas where reforms have the potential to stoke positive change and create a financial environment that is more inclusive, resilient, and in line with society's larger interests.

Administrative Changes: Enhanced Oversight and Enforcement for Stability and Fair Practices: Fortifying administrative bodies and furnishing them with the assets and authority expected to administer monetary organizations, guaranteeing consistence with guidelines and moral principles really.

Versatile Administrative Systems: Creating administrative systems that are dexterous and receptive to the developing monetary scene, including arising advancements, to dependably forestall administrative holes and cultivate development.

Straightforwardness Measures: Executing straightforwardness prerequisites that propel monetary foundations to uncover significant data, guaranteeing responsibility, and empowering shoppers to settle on informed choices.

Monetary Consideration Drives: Connecting Holes and Enabling People group

Fintech for Incorporation: Advancing the turn of events and reception of fintech arrangements that upgrade monetary access, especially in underserved networks, cultivating imaginative ways to deal with banking and installment frameworks.

Initiatives in Community Banking: Empowering the foundation of local area centered banks that focus on the necessities of nearby occupants and organizations, encouraging monetary development and lessening dependence on huge, brought together establishments.

Monetary Proficiency Projects: Executing thorough monetary training projects to engage people with the information and abilities expected to pursue informed choices, connecting the instruction partition and advancing mindful monetary practices.

Tending to Foundational Separation: Advancing Fairness and Variety

Variety and Consideration Strategies: Commanding monetary foundations to embrace and effectively authorize variety and incorporation approaches, guaranteeing fair portrayal at all levels and destroying fundamental segregation.

Hostile to segregation Guidelines: Fortifying enemy of segregation guidelines to address oppressive loaning rehearses, wage holes, and other foundational inclinations that sustain social and financial disparity.

Equivalent Open door Drives: Teaming up with instructive organizations and businesses to make pathways for underrepresented gatherings to get to open doors inside the monetary area, advancing correspondence of chance.

Reasonable Lodging Arrangements: Guaranteeing Safe house for All

Reasonable Lodging Projects: Executing and extending reasonable lodging drives that focus on the requirements of low and center pay people, encouraging manageable and comprehensive metropolitan turn of events.

Lease Control Measures: Acquainting rent control measures with alleviate lodging abberations, shield occupants from unreasonable lease increments, and advance steady and reasonable real estate markets.

Local area driven Advancement: Enabling people group to take part in dynamic cycles connected with lodging improvement, guaranteeing that activities meet the assorted requirements of the populace.

Corporate Social Obligation (CSR): Adjusting Benefit to Reason

Moral Speculation Practices: Empowering monetary organizations to embrace moral venture rehearses that think about natural, social, and administration (ESG) factors, adjusting speculation choices to more extensive cultural interests.

Local area Venture Projects: requiring financial institutions to donate a portion of their profits to community investment programs that support infrastructure, healthcare, education, and other local needs.

Partner Commitment: fostering increased stakeholder participation in decision-making processes to ensure that corporate actions reflect broader societal values, including customers, employees, and local communities.

Economic Equity through Global Collaboration: International Standards: A Unified Approach establishing and adhering to international standards for financial practices, taxation, and trade to prevent the exploitation of less developed economies and reduce global economic disparities.

Obligation Alleviation Projects: Carrying out fair and practical obligation help programs for emerging countries, lightening financial weights and advancing worldwide monetary strength.

Innovation Move Drives: Working with the exchange of innovation and information from created to creating economies, empowering them to take part more fairly in the worldwide monetary scene.

Conclusion: Graphing Another Course

The excursion toward a fair and impartial monetary future requires a cooperative and decided exertion. By carrying out these changes and arrangements, the monetary framework can develop into a power for positive cultural change. The quest for inclusivity, straightforwardness, and moral practices isn't just an ethical goal yet additionally an essential push toward building a versatile and economical monetary environment that benefits people, networks, and countries at large.

End

All in all, the complexities of the monetary framework, enveloping underlying issues, institutional disappointments, risk the executives challenges, conduct factors, globalization, government and strategy disappointments, mechanical dangers, and social and financial imbalance, require a nuanced and thorough way to deal with changes and arrangements. The interconnectedness of these issues and the need for a coordinated and adaptable response have been highlighted by this investigation.

Transforming the monetary framework requires a pledge to straightforwardness, moral practices, and inclusivity. Administrative changes should be coordinated, adjusting to mechanical headways and market elements. Reaching the unbanked and underbanked, as well as empowering individuals and communities, should be the top priority for financial inclusion initiatives. Endeavors to address foundational segregation and advance variety inside the monetary area are essential to cultivating a fair and impartial climate.

Reasonable lodging arrangements and corporate social obligation drives add to social and monetary prosperity, guaranteeing that the advantages of financial development are shared by different fragments of society. Worldwide, cooperation and global norms can assist with crossing over monetary incongruities and advance a more adjusted and interconnected monetary scene.

Innovation, while a wellspring of dangers, likewise offers valuable open doors for development and monetary incorporation. Utilizing arising advancements capably and guaranteeing powerful network protection measures are basic for exploring the computerized wilderness.

The contextual analyses of microfinance in Bangladesh, the Dodd-Candid Demonstration in the US, and M-Pesa in Kenya feature fruitful techniques and examples learned. Dodd-Frank demonstrates the significance of regulatory responses to crises, M-Pesa demonstrates how technology can transform financial inclusion, and microfinance demonstrates the power of small loans to empower individuals.

In graphing another course for the monetary future, the accentuation ought to be on moral practices, straightforwardness, and a promise to cultural prosperity. By encouraging a monetary framework that is versatile, comprehensive, and lined up with more extensive cultural interests, we can take a stab at a future where the advantages of financial thriving are shared fairly, enabling people and networks around the world.